READING GAMES WORKBOOK
FOR STRUGGLING READERS

READING GAMES

Workbook for Struggling Readers

101 Engaging Activities
to Develop Strong Reading Fluency
and Comprehension

CATHY HENRY, MS

Illustrations by Collaborate Agency

**ROCKRIDGE
PRESS**

For my three children,
who have all grown into readers.

First Rockridge Press trade paperback edition 2022

Rockridge Press and the Rockridge Press logo are trademarks or registered trademarks of Callisto Media Inc. and/or its affiliates in the United States and other countries and may not be used without written permission.

For general information on our other products and services, please contact our Customer Care Department within the United States at (866) 744-2665, or outside the United States at (510) 253-0500.

Paperback ISBN: 978-1-68539-969-6

Manufactured in the United States of America

Interior and Cover Designer: Alan Carr
Art Producer: Melissa Malinowksy
Editor: Annie Choi
Production Editor: Holland Baker and Rachel Taenzler
Production Manager: Lanore Coloprisco

Illustrations by Collaborate Agency

10 9 8 7 6 5 4 3 2 1 0

Contents

Introduction

Dear Families,

   Welcome to *Reading Games Workbook for Struggling Readers*, a fun way for your child to develop reading fluency and comprehension skills.

   As an elementary and special education teacher of 14 years, I am passionate about helping children discover the joy of reading. I get to see how everyone who enters my classroom gains skills and confidence as they become independent readers.

   This book is designed for children in grades 1 to 3. It is crucial to build strong reading skills at this age so kids can learn about the world around them. During this time, reading difficulties may also be first apparent. This book addresses skill gaps by allowing your child to practice reading and build confidence while having fun! There are 101 engaging, on-the-page activities that help build fluency by targeting four core skills: phonics, sight words, sentence structure, and reading comprehension.

   You can even go beyond this book by creating additional practice time in your routine. Take 10 to 15 minutes a day to read together. When you are out and about, practice reading by looking at signs, menus, and other printed materials in your environment. At breakfast, for example, you could put a cereal box in front of your child and give them words to hunt for. Also, be sure to surround them with books that are of high interest.

   My hope is that when your child completes the activities, they become a more confident, enthusiastic reader who finds the fun in reading. Let's get started!

How to Use This Book

The book is divided into four sections that explore phonics, sight words, sentence structure, and reading comprehension. The sections are color coded to make it easy to identify each type of skill. As the book progresses, your reader will find that more complex skills are gradually introduced, and the activities steadily increase in difficulty. This will help them build confidence over time.

If your child is a reluctant reader, be sure to encourage them along the way. The time they spend working on this book should be a positive experience. Reassure your child that they can ask for help when needed. If they struggle with any activity, read the directions aloud and point to the words. Next, have your child point at the same words and read them back to you. You will want to gauge their understanding before they begin working. If they need additional support, have them read the rest of the text on the page to you. Discuss the next steps together before working on the activity.

Remember that all children are unique, and everyone learns at their own pace. If it seems like your reader is becoming frustrated, it's okay to take a break. When they return to the activity, see what help you can offer for them to feel successful. If your child is motivated by small rewards, add a sticker to each page once it is completed.

Most important, remember that this book is supposed to be fun. Enjoy this time together!

Fun with Phonics

Vowels are the letters **A**, **E**, **I**, **O**, and **U**. Consonants are all the other letters in the alphabet. In this section, you will learn how to combine vowels and consonants to make new sounds. This is called phonics.

Phonics shows you how sounds and letters are related. This makes reading a lot more fun. Phonics will help you build other reading skills, too. You will read silent letters, longer words, and more. You will use these skills later in this book. Have fun learning to read new words!

Beginning Letter Sounds

Say the sound each letter makes. Draw a line from each letter to the picture that begins with the matching sound.

V

D

B

F

P

Z

N

M

Follow the Short Vowels

Vowels can make a short sound or a long sound. The **a** sound in **can** is short. The **a** sound in **day** is long. Follow the words with short vowel sounds to get through the maze.

Ending Sounds

An ending sound is the sound at the end of a word. Circle the words in each row with the same ending sound.

bad	top	hid	can
ten	fin	red	got
run	wet	pan	ship
fall	pet	bed	will
back	pick	fish	lap
push	pig	chip	wash

Blending Sounds

When you put letters together to make words, you are blending sounds. Blend the sounds to say each word. Write the word on the line. Draw a picture of each word inside the box.

Changing Sounds

Changing the letter in a word sometimes makes a new word. Follow the arrow to replace the underlined letters. Write the new word.

cap
↓
＿ ＿ n

hit
↓
＿ o ＿

top
↓
m ＿ ＿

big
↓
＿ ＿ t

six
↓
＿ ＿ p

fin
↓
＿ a ＿

pat
↓
＿ ＿ n

sun
↓
r ＿ ＿

Removing Sounds

Removing a letter from a word sometimes makes a new word. Take away the underlined letters and write the new word. Say each word.

scar → _____

ship → _____

twin → _____

stand → _____

black → _____

drip → _____

bring → _____

flake → _____

Color the Rhyming Words

Rhyming words sound the same at the end. The words **cat** and **bat** are rhyming words. They both end in the sound **-at**. Use the key to color the picture. What do you see?

Color Key

swim

wave

shell

book

spell

swell

well

cave

dwell

slim

him

save

brave

trim

tell

tell

brim

rave

save

well

skim

dwell

look

nook

took

Three in a Row

A blend is two or three consonants that make one sound. Draw a line through the words with the same beginning blend to make three in a row.

frog	from	friend	slide	play	glad
try	crib	write	grin	plate	prize
brick	black	drip	dress	plane	braid

cry	trick	dry	stop	snap	train
flag	drum	brown	clay	star	brush
draw	from	trip	grass	plant	stem

Reading Longer Words

Break longer words into parts so they are easier to read. The words below are broken into two parts. Read the parts to make the word. Then draw a line from each word to the matching picture.

pa – per

riv – er

15

wag – on

pump – kin

fif – teen

doc – tor

spi – der

mon – key

Color by Endings

A suffix is at the end of a word. Two suffixes are -**s** and -**ing**. Read each word. Use the key to color the picture.

Color Key

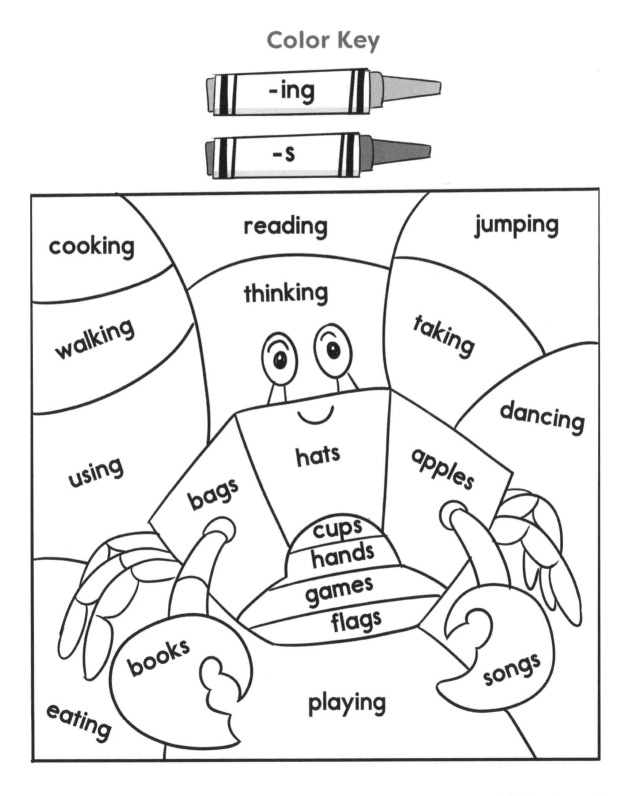

Count the Syllables

You can clap the beats in a word to find the syllables. Count the syllables in each word. Color the circle with the matching number.

fox   ① ② ③

anteater   ① ② ③

eagle   ① ② ③

cat   ① ② ③

bear   ① ② ③

lizard   ① ② ③

dog   ① ② ③

elephant   ① ② ③

owl   ① ② ③

A Day at the Beach

A digraph is two letters that make a new sound. The **sh** sound in **ship** is a digraph. Say each word and listen to the beginning sound. Circle the digraph at the beginning of each word.

shop

whale

cheese

think

phone

she

chop

when

Farm Search

When the letter **R** follows a vowel, it changes the sound the vowel makes. This is called an r-controlled vowel. Find and circle the words with r-controlled vowels in the puzzle.

Word Bank		
farm	shirt	turn
her	storm	hard

s	t	e	g	s	g	m	n
e	t	x	k	b	b	r	i
c	q	o	x	x	u	x	g
h	s	d	r	t	m	g	v
y	a	m	x	m	v	i	q
h	r	r	s	h	i	r	t
e	e	k	d	w	w	s	s
r	i	f	a	r	m	y	q

Magic E

When the letter **E** is silent at the end of a word, it is called a magic E. It makes the other vowel in the word a long vowel. Draw a line through the words with a magic E to make three in a row.

face	dust	sled	spot	ten	band
game	pig	box	mud	lick	club
made	cup	ball	fire	like	ride

wet	frog	clue	ask	mad	bone
mug	land	tube	bus	nose	flat
cub	pin	blue	home	dot	duck

Missing Vowel Teams

Two vowels can come together to make one vowel sound.
This is called a vowel team. Use the sound bank to write the
missing vowel team in each word.

Sound Bank		
ai	ee	oa

r__ __n   p__ __nt   t__ __l

tr__ __   d__ __r   thr__ __

b__ __t   c__ __t   s__ __p

R-Controlled Vowels

Say these words with r-controlled vowels: **dark**, **horse**, **fork**. Circle the word with the r-controlled vowel that matches each picture.

care / chair / curl	sure / curb / curl	burn / bird / third
hear / hard / hair	here / horse / hair	four / first / fair
girl / glare / gear	square / store / scar	park / pour / pair

Color by Digraphs

Some digraphs at the end of words are **ng**, **nk**, **ck**, **sh**, **th**, and **ch**. Use the key to color the picture.

Color Key

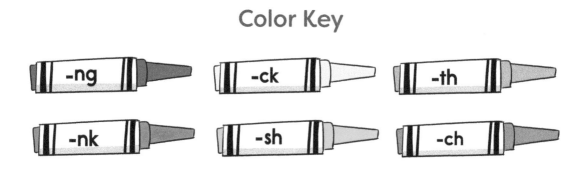

-ng   -ck   -th

-nk   -sh   -ch

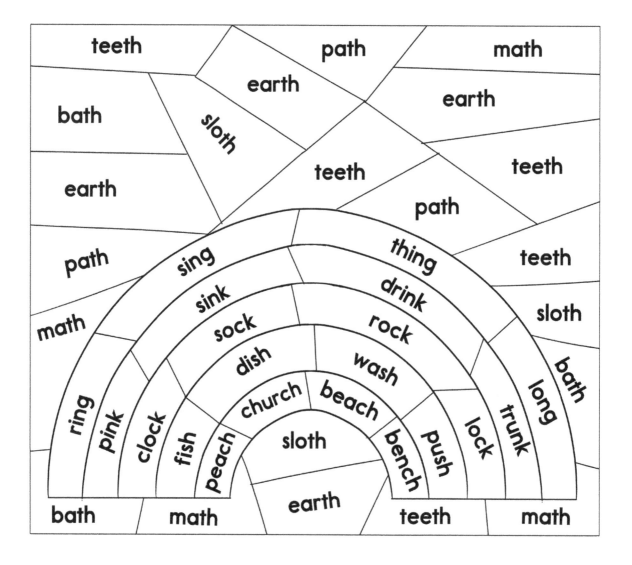

Soft C or Hard C?

A soft **C** makes the **s** sound. A hard **C** makes the **k** sound. Say each word. Listen for the hard **C** or soft **C**. Color the box with the matching sound.

camp	hard c
	soft c

care	hard c
	soft c

cold	hard c
	soft c

race	hard c
	soft c

pencil	hard c
	soft c

city	hard c
	soft c

corn	hard c
	soft c

cook	hard c
	soft c

place	hard c
	soft c

face	hard c
	soft c

Soft G and Hard G

A soft **G** makes the **j** sound, like the beginning of **giant**.
A hard **G** makes the **g** sound, like the beginning of **gum**.
Draw a line through the words with soft **G** or hard **G** to make three in a row.

bake	gift	then	best	magic	girl
look	fast	bag	log	gym	have
age	page	giant	did	giraffe	sand

huge	ball	gap	one	may	gas
come	goat	see	stage	blue	gift
gum	was	new	cut	hand	game

Trigraph Search

A trigraph has three letters that make one sound, like **str** in the word **strap**. Find and circle the words with trigraphs in the puzzle.

Word Bank

scrape	splash	string
screw	spray	stretch

o	w	o	v	y	s	n	s
r	g	w	a	c	x	d	p
s	t	r	e	t	c	h	l
x	p	a	m	r	n	r	a
s	p	s	c	r	e	w	s
s	c	r	a	p	e	t	h
o	w	p	b	w	o	b	d
s	t	r	i	n	g	h	i

Follow the Diphthongs

A diphthong is a set of letters that makes two vowel sounds. Help the dragon get to the castle! Follow the words with diphthongs **oy**, **ou**, or **ow**.

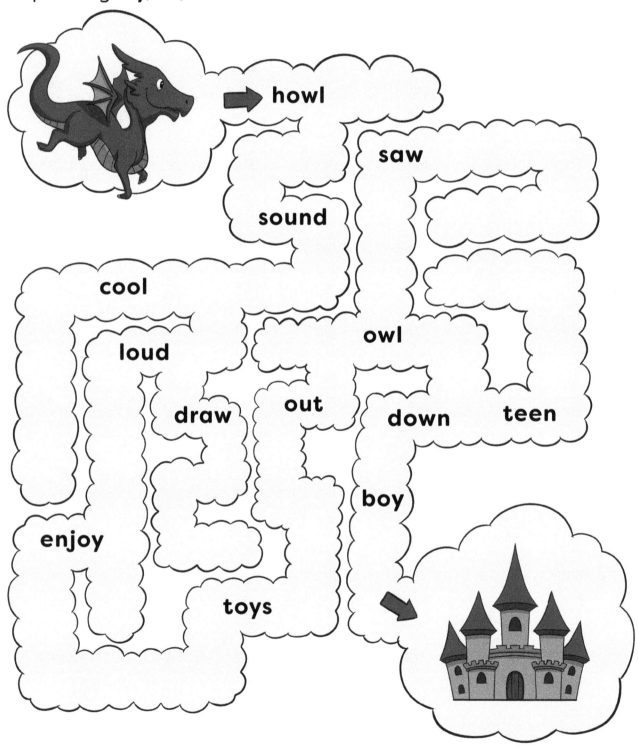

Double Consonants

Say these words with double consonants: **happy**, **puppy**, **penny**, **little**. Fill in the missing double consonants.

a__ __le

pi__ __a

ca__ __ot

ki__ __en

do__ __ar

le__ __er

fu__ __y

pu__ __le

Silent Letters

Silent letters are letters you do not hear when you say a word. Circle the words that have silent letters.

knock

fist

comb

walk

tree

half

drag

hour

bed

wrist

castle

What Sound?

The suffix **-ed** can sound like **t**, **d**, or **ed**. Say each word. Check the box with the matching **-ed** sound.

added	looked
○ t	○ t
○ d	○ d
○ ed	○ ed
wanted	**closed**
○ t	○ t
○ d	○ d
○ ed	○ ed
helped	**danced**
○ t	○ t
○ d	○ d
○ ed	○ ed
needed	**pulled**
○ t	○ t
○ d	○ d
○ ed	○ ed

Alliteration

Alliteration is when a group of words have the same beginning letter or sound. Read each sentence out loud. Write the beginning letter that is repeated.

Two turtles took turns.	

Six silly snakes slithered slowly.	

Five funny frogs flew far.	

My mom makes macaroni.	

We will walk with Wendy.	

Super Sight Words

Sight words are the words you see most when you read. They are sometimes called snap words or high-frequency words. When you do the activities in this section, you will read these words without sounding them out. This means you will know them on sight.

Most sight words do not have matching pictures. This includes words like **a**, **and**, or **the**. Some sight words are easier to picture in your mind, like **boy** and **farm**.

Get ready to have fun with sight words by doing the puzzles and games!

Sight Word Search

Sight words are the most common words you read and write. Find and circle the sight words in the puzzle.

Word Bank		
this	we	than
as	she	been

o	a	w	q	x	n	y	q
i	s	h	e	b	d	y	a
t	q	m	w	e	o	p	x
z	h	o	c	e	x	f	t
t	a	i	z	n	z	t	t
r	h	p	s	p	s	q	a
u	l	a	k	m	o	f	r
b	x	g	n	x	c	e	p

Tic-Tac-Toe

Some sight words only have two letters. Draw a line through the matching sight words to make three in a row.

of	to	buy
we	of	he
is	or	of

up	by	is
in	in	in
he	be	of

he	it	of
in	it	if
so	it	be

as	at	on
an	on	it
on	do	or

Let's Go Skating!

Learning sight words will help you read. Help the skater get to the medal. Follow the sight words **more**, **there**, and **an**.

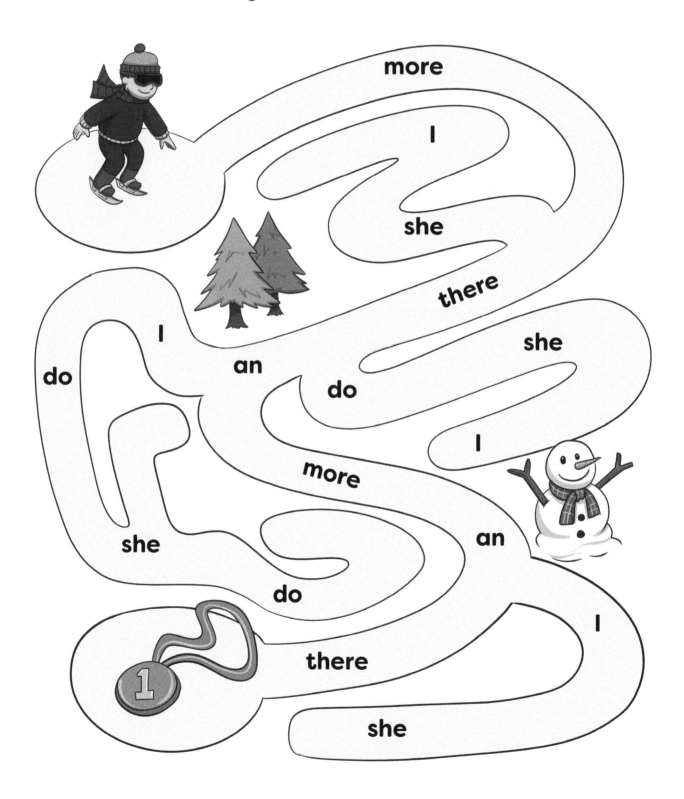

X Marks the Spot!

Consonants are letters that are not **A**, **E**, **I**, **O**, or **U**. Draw an **X** on the sight words that start with a consonant.

Blast Off!

You learn sight words by memorizing them. That means you don't have to sound them out. Use the key to color the picture.

Color Key

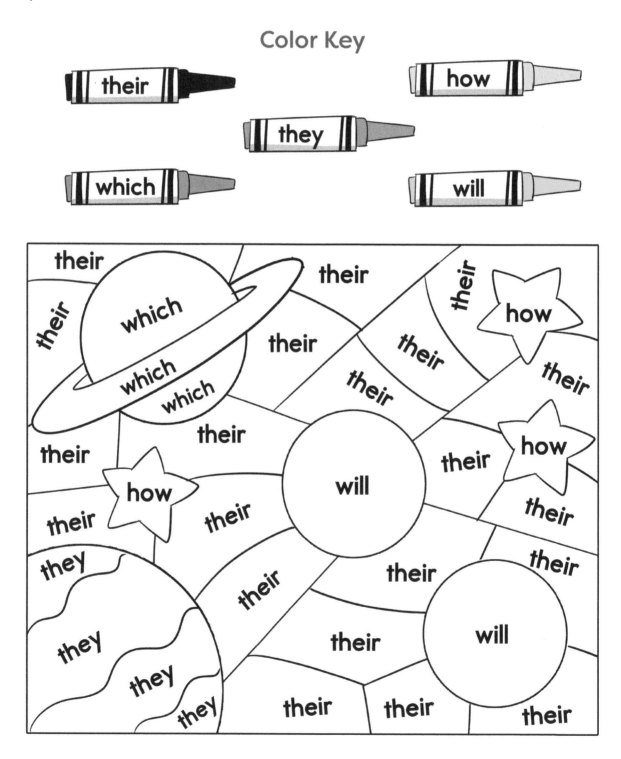

Trace and Match

Sight words can be tricky to spell. Tracing the letters can help you remember the spelling. Trace the words. Circle the matching word in each row.

one	he	one	was
had	with	can	had
by	by	for	at
word	and	this	word
but	all	but	she
not	how	not	do
what	what	your	of
all	each	from	all

Find the Hidden Words

Reading a word over and over can help you memorize it. Use the word bank to find and circle the words.

Word Bank		
other	many	people
about	number	them

Find the Vowels

Most words have at least one vowel. Some have more than one. Vowels are the letters **A**, **E**, **I**, **O**, and **U**. Circle the vowels in each word.

part   made

come   get

down   long

find   called

been   water

Missing Letters

Pictures can help you remember words. Look at each picture. Say the word. Fill in the missing letter.

rea ___

___lock

___ook

firs ___

___ack

___oy

Rainy Day Maze

Most syllables have only one vowel sound. Follow the words with one syllable to find your way home.

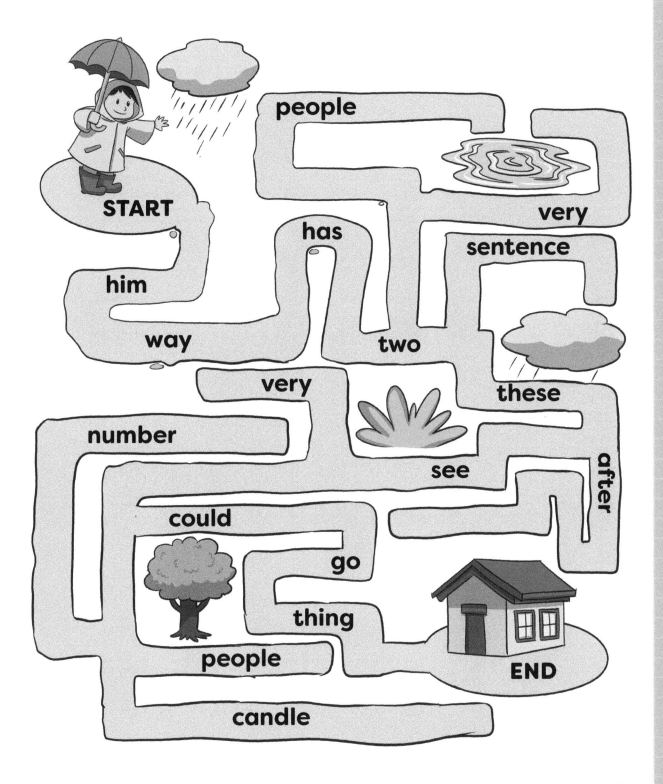

START

people

very

has

sentence

him

way

two

these

very

number

see

after

could

go

thing

people

END

candle

Scrambled Words

The letters in a scrambled word are mixed up in a different order. Use the word bank to unscramble the letters. Write the word.

tsju   _____

kowr   _____

nwok   _____

Word Bank
must
help
know
just
work
want
name
same

mena   _____

lhep   _____

ames   _____

nwat   _____

sutm   _____

Consonants in a Row

The most common consonants are **L**, **N**, **R**, **S**, and **T**. Draw a line through the words with the same beginning consonant to make three in a row.

by	for	try	that	can	say
your	tell	at	what	part	small
too	I	each	my	an	set

or	if	into	am	number	other
live	land	line	day	now	its
so	did	all	up	new	may

In the Desert

You read and write numbers, not just words. Look at the picture. Count how many times you find each word. Write the number.

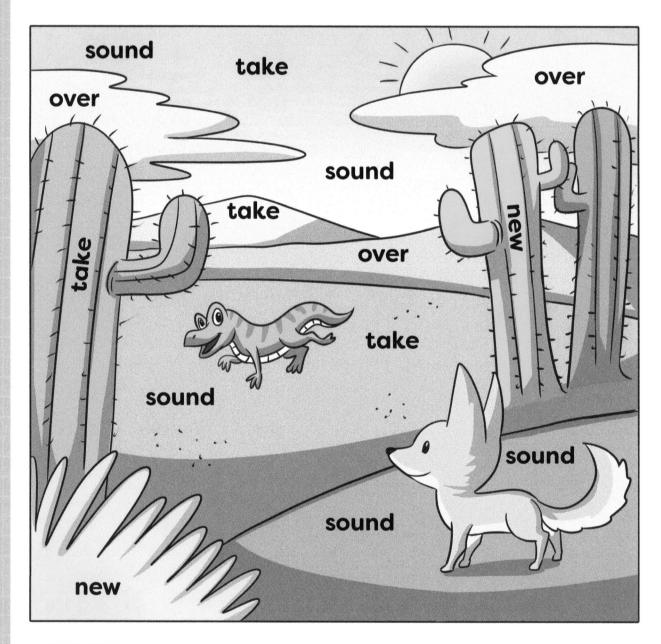

over	new	sound	take

Picture Match

You can draw a picture of some sight words. Draw a line from each picture to the matching sight word.

world

house

man

three

farm

water

letter

Color the Picture

You can remember sight words by reading them over and over. Use the key to color the picture. What do you see?

Color Key

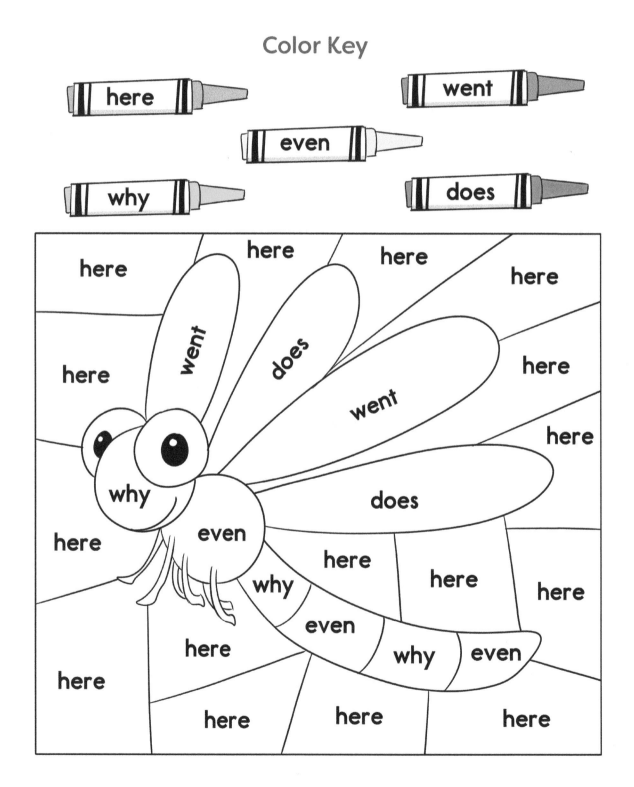

Count the Syllables

You can clap the beats in a word to count the syllables. Say each word. Count the syllables. Circle the matching number.

study			spell	
1	2		1	2

mother			letters	
1	2		1	2

because			should	
1	2		1	2

still			air	
1	2		1	2

answer			off	
1	2		1	2

What Does It Mean?

Words are put together to make sentences. Draw a line from each sentence to the matching picture.

I will take one cookie.

She is five years old.

He wrote a word.

There is a farm.

I found the animals.

There are three small boys.

What Is Missing?

After you write a sentence, read it again to check that it makes sense. What word belongs in each sentence? Use the word bank to fill in the blanks.

Word Bank		
think	Where	through
following	little	good

_____ will we go?

I will walk _____the door.

What do you _____?

The puppy is _____ me.

This is a _____ idea.

The baby bird is _____.

Sight Word Check

As you learn more sight words, you become an even better reader. Read the sight words. Circle the words you know. Memorize any words you do not know.

came	read	also	tell
line	then	some	great
old	any	before	help
want	show	around	means

Find the Sight Words

When you learn a new sight word, ask an adult to help you say it. Find and circle the sight words in the puzzle.

Word Bank		
earn	page	away
kind	point	play

r	p	l	a	y	h	w	o
v	s	n	i	r	h	a	q
c	k	i	n	d	e	e	y
y	e	f	a	w	a	y	a
l	x	g	e	a	r	n	d
r	p	o	i	n	t	v	p
d	p	w	l	h	t	x	b
w	h	a	h	p	a	g	e

Vowels in a Row

Vowels are the letters **A**, **E**, **I**, **O**, and **U**. Draw a line through the sight words beginning with vowels to make three in a row.

that	was	end	can	we	if
he	even	had	which	by	air
off	from	with	not	she	again
this	words	but	answer	its	only
away	out	into	this	how	do
to	have	his	their	your	when

Scrambled Sentences

Words are the building blocks of a sentence. Unscramble and write the sentences.

to went farm. the I

_____

are The different. animals

_____

found I picture. a

_____

another I see house.

_____

is The cookie large.

_____

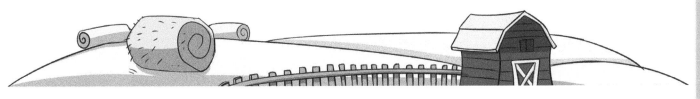

Choose the Missing Word

You can read a sentence out loud to see if it makes sense. Read each sentence. Circle the missing word.

She **and** / **found** / **home** the book.

I used a **play** / **land** / **different** color.

They walked **around** / **world** / **hand** the park.

I **asked** / **still** / **again** for help.

He took a **went** / **picture** / **end**.

Do you feel **think** / **know** / **well**?

What Do You See?

You can show the meaning of a sentence with pictures. Draw a picture that matches each sentence.

The house is blue.

The boy can read.

I see the animals.

I write a sentence.

Building Fluency

Use the word bank to write the missing word in each sentence. Read the sentences out loud until you are reading with fluency.

Word Bank		
America	us	again
change	went	following

I watched the movie _____.

He will _____ his shirt.

The cat was _____ us.

This is a map of _____.

Will you come with _____?

I _____ down the slide.

Building Sentences

When you learn how sentences work, reading becomes more fun! This section is about building sentences. You will learn what a complete sentence looks like. You will learn about the different parts of speech, like nouns, verbs, and adjectives. You will also see how writers put words together to make sentences. Then you will build and write your own sentences. Enjoy the games and activities!

Is It a Sentence?

A complete sentence will tell you what it is about and what is happening. Circle **yes** if the sentence is complete. Circle **no** if it is not a complete sentence.

my friend	**yes**	**no**
We went to the park.	**yes**	**no**
Played soccer.	**yes**	**no**
The kids	**yes**	**no**
They played tag.	**yes**	**no**
We had a picnic.	**yes**	**no**

Capitalize It!

A sentence always begins with a capital letter. Circle the letter that should be capitalized.

let's go to the gym!

we will play basketball.

did you bring a basketball?

there are four kids on our team.

who made a basket?

we won the game!

Add the Ending

Punctuation marks have different uses. A period (.) is for a statement. A question mark (?) is for a question. An exclamation point (!) shows strong feeling. Add the right punctuation mark to complete each sentence.

Can we go to the zoo _____

I am so excited to see the animals _____

There are monkeys and lions _____

We can watch the zookeeper feed the seals _____

What time is the bird show _____

Follow the Nouns

A noun is a person, place, or thing. Follow the nouns to help the turtle find the pond.

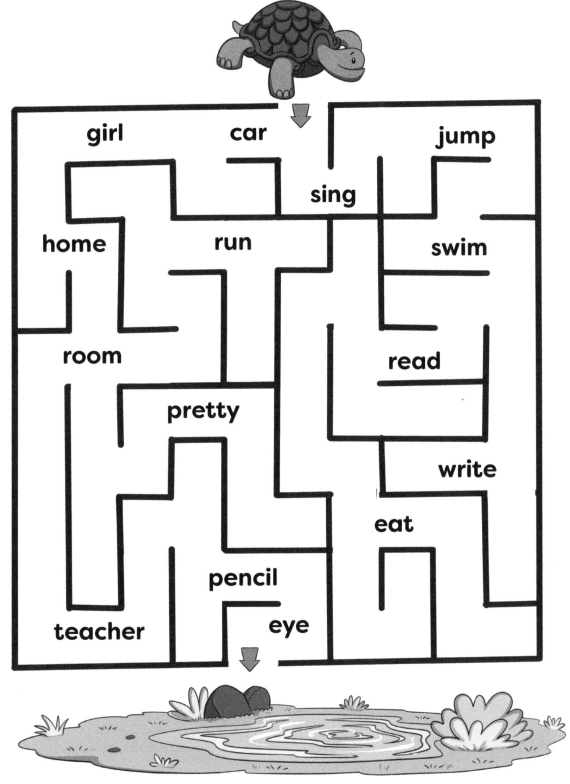

Which Pronoun?

A pronoun is a short word that can replace a noun. Some pronouns are **he**, **she**, **it**, and **they**. Circle the pronoun that completes each sentence.

Us / **We** will go to the library.

Her / **She** will read us a story.

Can **I** / **me** get a new book?

This is **my** / **mine** favorite book.

Today **him** / **he** will try a new book.

They / **Them** will go to the library tomorrow.

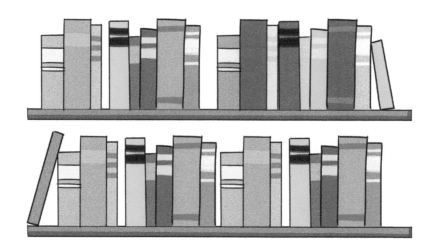

Baking Up Verbs

A verb is an action word. It tells you what someone is doing or what is happening. Find and circle the verbs in the picture.

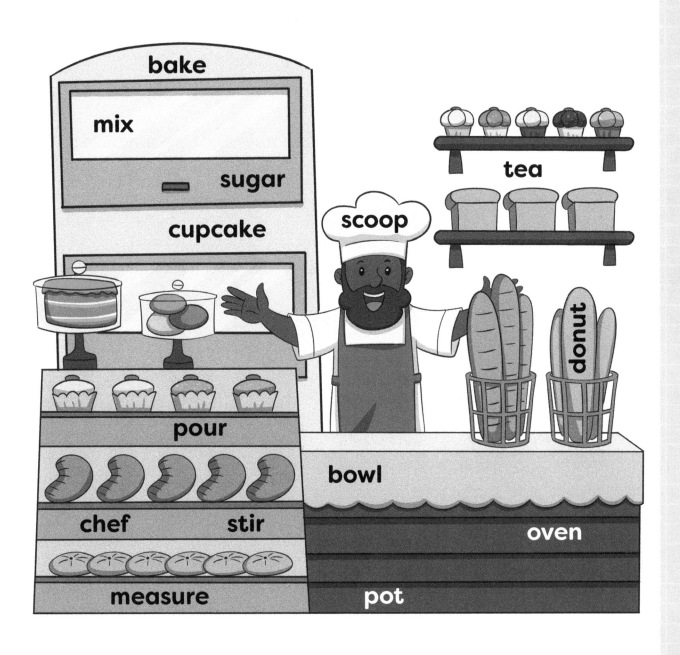

Find the Adjectives

An adjective is a word that describes a noun. Find and circle the adjectives in the puzzle.

Word Bank

brown	tiny	playful
furry	friendly	quick

a	c	w	t	n	i	l	f
x	d	n	w	i	u	p	r
j	q	o	b	f	n	u	i
j	r	s	y	r	u	y	e
b	v	a	u	p	j	b	n
f	l	f	u	r	r	y	d
p	q	u	i	c	k	k	l
m	o	z	y	f	v	s	y

Connect the Verbs

An action verb describes an action. Some action verbs are **run**, **smile**, and **take**. Draw a line through the action verbs to make three in a row.

big	shoe	bus	make	happy	bug
cook	swim	work	climb	fast	book
car	purple	loud	talk	bird	green
blue	flower	clap	bed	cup	red
coat	pull	rainy	clue	shoe	small
write	ice	tree	cry	give	drop

Where Is the Cat?

A preposition can tell you where something is. Use the word bank to fill in the blanks. Write the missing word that matches the picture.

The cat is _____ the box.

The cat is _____ the box.

The cat is _____ the box.

Word Bank

inside

beside

under

above

behind

on

The cat is _____ the box.

The cat is _____ the box.

The cat is _____ the box.

Describe It!

Adjectives can describe what something looks like. For example, an apple is red and round. Write two adjectives that describe each picture.

_____

_____

_____

_____

My New Bike

Write the missing word in each sentence. Use the word bank to fill in the blanks.

Word Bank		
wear	got	bike
fast	ride	

I _____ a new bike for my birthday.

Let's _____ our bikes together.

Make sure you _____ a helmet!

My _____ has two pedals.

How _____ can you pedal?

Let's Clean!

A sentence makes sense when the words are in order.
Unscramble and write the sentences.

messy. My room is

_____

clean room. I my will

_____

help Will me? you

_____

stack my I books. will

_____

basket. clothes The in the go

_____

clean! my Look at room

_____

Color the Nouns

A proper noun is a word that names a person, place, or thing. It begins with a capital letter. Use the key to color the picture.

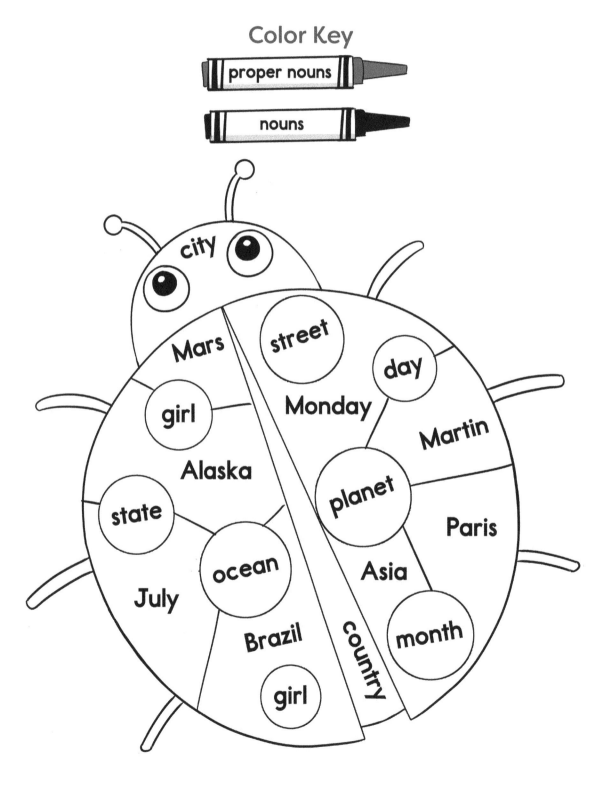

Am, Is, or Are?

The verb **to be** can be written as **am**, **is**, or **are**. Use **am** when you talk about yourself. Use **is** for one thing or person. Use **are** for more than one thing or person. The sentences are missing a verb. Use the word bank to write the missing verb.

Word Bank
am   is   are

Today _____ my birthday.

I _____ having a party.

My friends _____ coming over.

It _____ almost time.

They _____ on their way.

I _____ so excited!

Plural Nouns

A noun is one person, place, or thing. A plural noun is more than one. Draw a line through the plural nouns to make three in a row.

buses	key	butter	balloon	candy	mice
feet	spoon	wall	sister	cups	bear
people	boat	cheese	days	zebra	branch
bee	apple	birds	glass	bunny	dance
slide	box	leaves	horses	children	teeth
map	mouse	pencils	table	teacher	monkey

Sort the Words

A part of speech is a category of words. Nouns, verbs, and adjectives are parts of speech. Draw a line under the nouns. Draw an **X** on the verbs. Circle the adjectives.

chicken	doctor	listen	sister
home	blond	curvy	dirty
fluffy	hungry	odd	buy
write	carry	grape	like

Volcano Maze

Reading can help you learn new things. Follow the words that make a sentence to reach the top of the volcano.

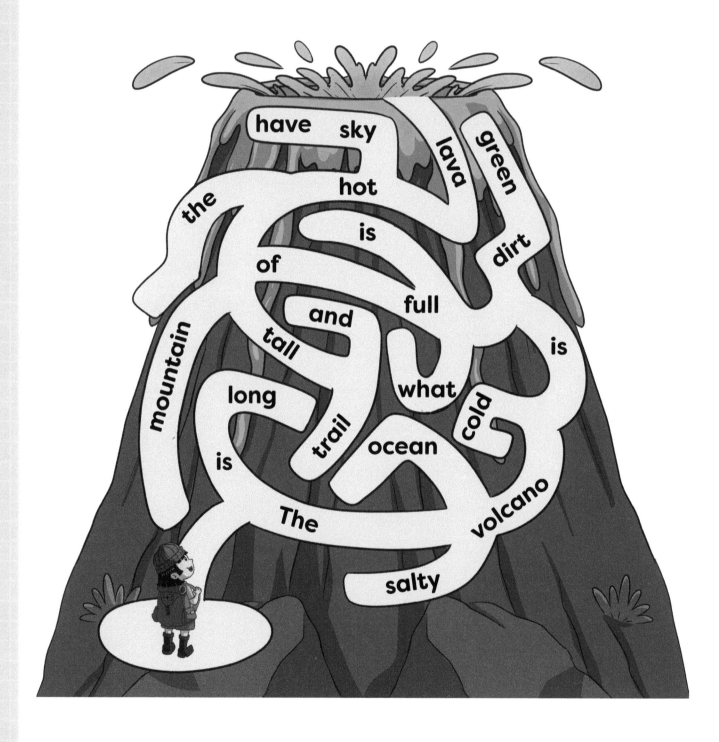

Building Better Sentences

You can use adjectives to give sentences more details. Use the word bank to complete each sentence.

Word Bank		
tired	yellow	noisy
tall	many	

1. There are _____ workers at the construction site.

2. They are building a _____ skyscraper.

3. I like watching the _____ trucks.

4. The machines are very _____, so the workers wear ear plugs.

5. The workers are _____ at the end of a hard day's work.

Cause and Effect

A cause is why something happens. An effect is what happened. Read each sentence. Write a sentence to describe the effect.

Cause	Effect
Example: *I was very hungry.*	*I ate a sandwich.*
I hurt my arm at basketball.	_____
I got a book at the library.	_____
I fell in the mud.	_____

Sentence Parts

Each part of a sentence tells you something. Draw lines to connect the matching parts of each sentence.

Who	**What**	**Where**
My teacher	are at the art table	playing games
The Magician	is at school	setting up the carnival
I	am at the carnival	making a painting.
My friends	is at the gym with his hat	doing magic tricks

Scrambled Sentences

A sentence always ends with a punctuation mark. Unscramble and write the sentences.

do like best? sport What you

_____

play friends. with softball I my

_____

called team My Lions. the is

_____

the field. ball the I hit into will

_____

you ball? catch the Can

_____

won yesterday! team game Our the

_____

Let's Go Fishing

A group of sentences can tell a story. Make a story about fishing. Circle the word that completes each sentence.

We went **skating** / **hiking** / **fishing** at the pond.

We used **worms** / **books** / **toys** for bait.

How many fish do you think we **caught** /
told / **ran**?

We had to be **loud** / **quiet** / **happy** so we did not
scare the fish.

We had a fun **party** / **breakfast** / **day**!

Music Class

You can read a sentence again to see if it makes sense. Use the word bank to complete each sentence. Read each sentence again. Does it make sense?

Word Bank		
teacher	play	learning
today	music	

Today we have _____ class.

The _____ tells us what to play.

I love _____ a new song each week.

Some days we get to _____ instruments.

I wonder what we will do _____ !

Cookout Fun!

A subject tells you who or what a sentence is about. A predicate tells you what happens. Draw a line from each subject to the matching predicate.

Subject	Predicate
My whole family	is full of tasty foods.
The kids	will go to a big cookout.
The picnic table	is red and juicy.
The watermelon	want to play games.

Compound Scramble

A compound sentence has more than one predicate. The word **and** can be used to connect the predicates. Unscramble the predicates to write the compound sentences.

kicked I ball the   and   made goal. a

_____   and   _____ .

dad My up woke   and   still sleepy. was

_____   and   _____ .

We movie watched a   and   ending. liked the

_____   and   _____ .

made toast She   and   it. ate

_____   and   _____ .

I Can Read!

Congratulations! You made it to the last section of the book! Now you can put together everything you have learned. In this section, you will practice reading by using phonics, sight words, and sentences. The fun activities build on these skills so you can solve problems with words. You will also draw pictures of what you read. The last activities ask you questions and make you think about what happens next in a story. You are on your way to becoming an even better reader!

What Am I?

A riddle gives you clues to find an answer. Draw a line from each riddle to the matching picture.

I am gray. I have a fluffy tail.
I live in a tree.

I am red. I live in a tree.
I can fly.

I am green. I might live
by a pond. I can hop.

I am long and skinny.
My skin is scaly.

I am orange and black.
I begin as a caterpillar.
I can fly.

Follow the Directions

A color word is the name of a color. Read each sentence with color words. Follow the directions to color the picture.

Color Key

Color two fish red.

Color one shell blue.

Color three starfish yellow.

Color two shells green.

Color one fish orange.

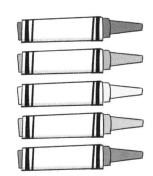

What Do You See?

Words and pictures can be used to tell a story. Read about the flower garden. Draw a picture to show what you read.

The garden is growing! I see three red flowers and two yellow flowers. There is a purple butterfly flying above the garden. I found a caterpillar crawling on green leaves. It is fun to look at the garden!

At the Zoo

As you read a story, each sentence tells you something new. Read each sentence. Draw a line to match it with the picture.

The children rode the bus to the zoo.

At the zoo, they saw the monkeys.

There were two lions in a cage.

I saw a zebra on the hill.

There were many flamingos.

Gray Wolves

A true statement is correct or right. A false statement is incorrect or wrong. Read about the gray wolf, then read the statements that follow. Write **true** or **false** next to each statement.

> Have you ever seen a gray wolf? The gray wolf can be gray, brown, black, or even white! The colors help the wolf hide in nature. Gray wolves hunt at night. They work together as a pack to hunt bigger animals.

_____ A gray wolf is always gray.

_____ The gray wolf can hunt at night.

_____ The colors make it hard for the wolf to hide.

_____ Gray wolves only hunt small animals.

Making Connections

When you read something new, you can connect it to something you already know. Read about the apple orchard. Use the questions to help you write about your own connection to the story.

> Our class went on a field trip to the apple orchard. The workers taught us how they grow the trees. We got to pick apples. We even tasted apples!
> My favorite apple was red and sweet.

Have you been to an apple orchard?

_____

Have you gone on a field trip?

_____

Do you like apples?

_____

Main Idea

The main idea of a story tells you what the story is about. Read the story about llamas. Think about the main idea as you read.

> Llamas are very smart animals. They can be trained to do many things. Llamas can learn to pull a cart. They help farmers carry heavy things. Llamas also work as guard animals.

The main idea is:

_____

_____

_____

_____

_____

_____

_____

_____

_____

What You Know

Background knowledge is what you already know before you read. Use your background knowledge about butterflies. Write what you already know about them. Then read the story that follows to an adult.

What I know about butterflies:

_____

_____

_____

_____

Amy loves to watch butterflies! They are her favorite insect. She likes how they start as a caterpillar and become a butterfly. Do you have a favorite insect?

_____

_____

_____

_____

Name That Food

Riddles are sometimes called brain teasers. This is because you use your brain to solve them. Draw a line to match each riddle with the picture.

I am baked in the oven.
I have cheese and tomato sauce.

I am yellow. I have a peel.

I am round and sweet.
I have a hole in the middle.

I am a fruit. I am red and crunchy.

I am made from potatoes.
I am salty and crispy.

I have a tortilla on the outside.
I have meat and beans.

What Will Damian Do?

A prediction is when you use clues to guess what will happen. Read about Damian. Make a prediction about what will happen.

Damian looked outside. It was snowing! He put on his coat, boots, gloves, and a hat. He found his sled in the garage. Then he walked up the hill next to his house.

What do you think Damian will do next?

_____

_____

_____

_____

_____

_____

_____

_____

Getting Ready

When you do not know a word, you can ask an adult for help. Read about the road trip. Circle any words you do not know and ask an adult. Then read the passage out loud.

> My family woke up early to get ready for our road trip. First, we packed our bags. Next, we packed a cooler with food. We put everything into the car. It was time to start our adventure!

Giant Pandas

A fact is a statement that can be proven true or false. An opinion is a belief or feeling. Opinions are not true or false. Read each statement. Write **F** if it is a fact. Write **O** if it is an opinion.

_____ Giant pandas are so fun to watch!

_____ They are a type of bear.

_____ Giant pandas are found in China.

_____ Their diet is mostly bamboo.

_____ All zoos should have giant pandas.

A Trip to the Ice Cream Shop

Sequencing is when you put sentences in order to tell a story. Read each sentence. Write the numbers **1** to **5** to put the sentences in order.

_____ She put the ice cream scoop on a cone.

_____ She handed me the cone.

_____ I ordered chocolate ice cream.

_____ I tasted the ice cream, and it was delicious!

_____ The worker scooped the ice cream.

Making Predictions

Words are clues that help you make a prediction. Read the story. Write one or two sentences to predict what will happen next.

> My mom told me to get my swimsuit and sunglasses. She put sunscreen on me and my brother. We put towels, buckets, and shovels in the car.

_____

_____

_____

_____

_____

_____

_____

_____

The Purpose of Writing

Writing has different purposes. It can **entertain**, **persuade**, and **inform**. Entertain is when you amuse. Persuade is when you to try to make someone believe an idea. Inform is when you teach. Why would the author write each of these books? Fill in the circle next to the matching purpose.

The Magical Unicorn
- ○ entertain
- ○ persuade
- ○ inform

Why You Should Play Basketball
- ○ entertain
- ○ persuade
- ○ inform

All about Penguins
- ○ entertain
- ○ persuade
- ○ inform

Desert Animals
- ○ entertain
- ○ persuade
- ○ inform

The Birthday Party Adventure
- ○ entertain
- ○ persuade
- ○ inform

Why You Should Get a Cat
- ○ entertain
- ○ persuade
- ○ inform

Learn by Reading

Reading can help us learn about the world. Read about the maned sloth. Write **true** or **false** next to the statements that follow.

The maned sloth lives in Brazil. It has thick, brown hair. Sloths like hot and humid weather. They live in trees where they can sleep up to 20 hours each day! Their favorite food is leaves.

True or False?

_____ The maned sloth has brown hair.

_____ The maned sloth likes snowy weather.

_____ The maned sloth only sleeps three hours a day.

_____ The maned sloth likes to eat leaves.

The Walk

Words can be shown in pictures. Read the story. Draw a picture to show what happened in the story.

> When I went for a walk with my sister, I saw a bird in a tree. The bird was big and blue. It was sitting in a nest. There were four tiny eggs in the nest. I loved watching the bird on this sunny day!

Reading Vocabulary

You learn different skills when you read. Draw a line from each reading skill to the matching definition.

prediction   the reason an
                                    author writes

fact   a belief

purpose   when a reader uses
                                    clues to figure out what
                                    will happen next

connection   being able to
                                    read easily

opinion   when we use what
                                    we already know to
                                    help us read

fluency   a statement that
                                    can be proven

Where Am I?

Reading and answering riddles can be like solving a mystery. Use the word bank to answer the riddles.

Word Bank		
school	forest	beach
zoo	desert	

_____ I have sand and salty water.

_____ I have many animals. They might live in cages or behind a fence.

_____ I have lots of trees. You can find birds, squirrels, and deer in me.

_____ I am very dry. You might see a cactus or a snake if you visit me.

_____ You will see books, pencils, and teachers here.

Narwhals

A paragraph is a group of sentences. Read about narwhals. Then read the questions. Underline the answers in the paragraph. Write the answers.

> A narwhal is a whale. It has a tusk on its head. This makes narwhals look like unicorns that swim! Narwhals live in icy ocean waters. They eat fish, shrimp, and squid.

What makes a narwhal look like a unicorn?

_____

Where do narwhals live?

_____

What are two foods that narwhals eat?

_____

Baking Cupcakes

When you bake, you follow the steps in a recipe. You have to follow the steps in order. Reading is the same. Words make sense when they are in order. Read each sentence. Write the numbers **1** to **5** to put the recipe in order.

_____ Stir the ingredients to make a batter.

_____ Spread icing on the cupcakes.

_____ Pour the batter into the cupcake pan.

_____ Bake the cupcakes.

_____ Pour the ingredients into a bowl.

Why Did the Author Write This?

Read about Power Shoes. Think about why this was written.

> Have you seen Power Shoes? They are the best shoes you will ever own. They will help you jump high and run fast. Plus, they look great. You should buy a pair today!

Why do you think the author wrote this?

_____

_____

_____

_____

_____

_____

_____

_____

Retelling a Story

A story has a beginning, middle, and end. Read the story about a camping trip. Draw pictures to show the beginning, middle, and end of the story.

> Kendall and Carter are going camping! First, they will pitch their tent. Next, they will build a campfire. Finally, they are going to cook dinner. They will have a fun night!

Beginning

Middle

End

Making a Summary

A summary tells the main idea of a story. Read the paragraph. Make a summary of what you read by explaining the main idea and writing three details.

My class went to the museum on our field trip. My favorite part of the museum had dinosaur fossils. We talked with a paleontologist. A paleontologist is a scientist who learns about dinosaurs by studying fossils. We learned that dinosaurs are reptiles that lived a long time ago. Did you know that some dinosaurs had feathers like birds? I learned so much on our trip!

What is the main idea?

_____

_____

Write three details.

1. _____

2. _____

3. _____

Let's Grow a Garden!

Read the paragraph about Ava and James below. Then read the questions that follow. Go back to the paragraph and underline the answers. Write the answers.

Ava and James are planting a garden at their school. They will grow fruits and vegetables to share with their class. Their friends will help them water the plants and pull out the weeds. They are excited about this new project!

Where are Ava and James planting a garden?

_____

What will they grow?

_____

What are two things that other people will help them do?

_____

Fun at the Park!

Multiple-choice questions give different options for answers. Read every answer before you pick one. Read the story, then circle the correct answers.

Eliana is meeting her friends at the park after school. Everyone is bringing a snack to share, then they will play together. Eliana's favorite game is tag. Her friend Zola likes the swings, and Ari likes to climb trees.

What is this story mostly about?

A. going to the zoo

B. going to the park

C. going to the museum

What is Eliana's favorite game to play at the park?

A. hopscotch

B. tag

C. hide and seek

Who likes to swing?

A. Ari

B. Eliana

C. Zola

When will Eliana and her friends go to the park?

A. after school

B. the weekend

C. before school

What will the friends do before they play?

A. ride bikes

B. run a race

C. eat a snack

What do you think Ari will ask to do first?

A. play tag

B. swing

C. climb

Answer Key

Beginning Letter Sounds

Say the sound each letter makes. Draw a line from each letter to the picture that begins with the matching sound.

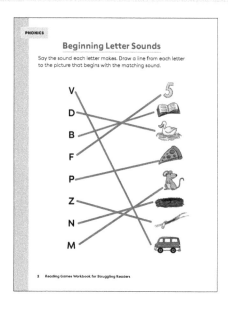

Follow the Short Vowels

Vowels can make a short sound or a long sound. The **a** sound in **can** is short. The **a** sound in **day** is long. Follow the words with short vowel sounds to get through the maze.

Ending Sounds

An ending sound is the sound at the end of a word. Circle the words in each row with the same ending sound.

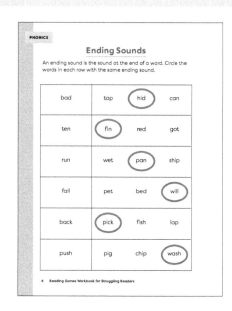

bad	top	hid	can
ten	fin	red	got
run	wet	pan	ship
fall	pet	bed	will
back	pick	fish	lap
push	pig	chip	wash

Blending Sounds

When you put letters together to make words, you are blending sounds. Blend the sounds to say each word. Write the word on the line. Draw a picture of each word inside the box.

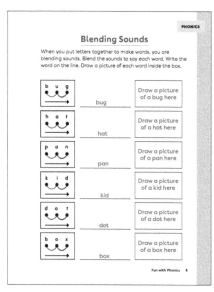

Changing Sounds

Changing the letter in a word sometimes makes a new word. Follow the arrow to replace the underlined letters. Write the new word.

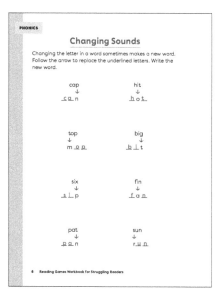

```
cap              hit
 ↓                ↓
c a n            h o t

top              big
 ↓                ↓
m o p            b i t

six              fin
 ↓                ↓
s i p            f a n

pat              sun
 ↓                ↓
p a n            r u n
```

Removing Sounds

Removing a letter from a word sometimes makes a new word. Take away the underlined letters and write the new word. Say each word.

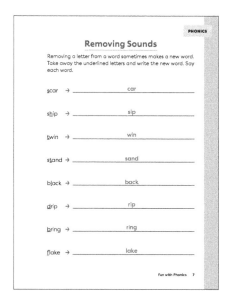

scar → car

ship → sip

twin → win

stand → sand

black → back

drip → rip

bring → ring

flake → lake

Color the Rhyming Words

Rhyming words sound the same at the end. The words **cat** and **bat** are rhyming words. They both end in the sound **-at**. Use the key to color the picture. What do you see?

Color Key

swim   shell
wave   book

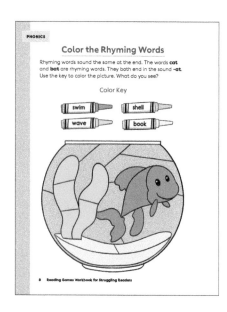

Three in a Row

A blend is two or three consonants that make one sound. Draw a line through the words with the same beginning blend to make three in a row.

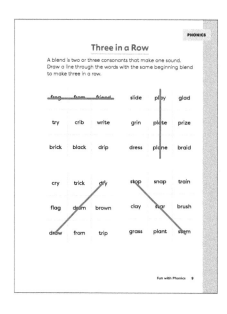

frog	from	friend	slide	play	glad
try	crib	write	grin	plate	prize
brick	black	drip	dress	plane	braid
cry	trick	dry	stop	snap	train
flag	drum	brown	clay	star	brush
draw	from	trip	grass	plant	stem

Reading Longer Words

Break longer words into parts so they are easier to read. The words below are broken into two parts. Read the parts to make the word. Then draw a line from each word to the matching picture.

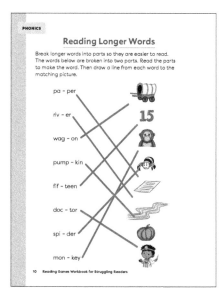

pa - per

riv - er

wag - on

pump - kin

fif - teen

doc - tor

spi - der

mon - key

Color by Endings

A suffix is at the end of a word. Two suffixes are -s and -ing. Read each word. Use the key to color the picture.

Color Key

-ing

-s

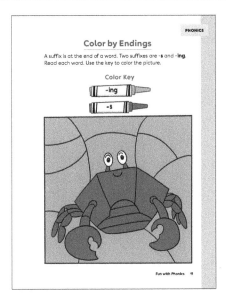

Count the Syllables

You can clap the beats in a word to find the syllables. Count the syllables in each word. Color the circle with the matching number.

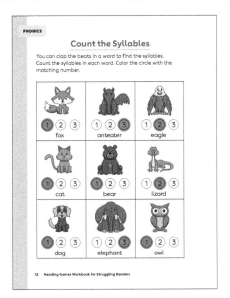

A Day at the Beach

A digraph is two letters that make a new sound. The **sh** sound in **ship** is a digraph. Say each word and listen to the beginning sound. Circle the digraph at the beginning of each word.

Farm Search

When the letter **R** follows a vowel, it changes the sound the vowel makes. This is called an r-controlled vowel. Find and circle the words with r-controlled vowels in the puzzle.

Word Bank

| farm | shirt | turn |
| her | storm | hard |

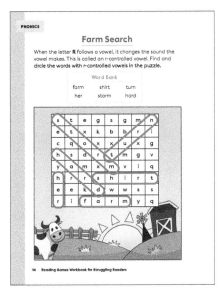

Magic E

When the letter **E** is silent at the end of a word, it is called a magic E. It makes the other vowel in the word a long vowel. Draw a line through the words with a magic E to make three in a row.

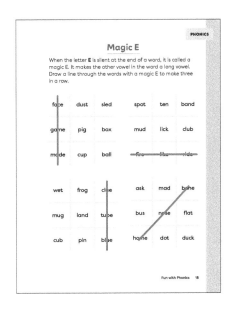

Missing Vowel Teams

Two vowels can come together to make one vowel sound. This is called a vowel team. Use the sound bank to write the missing vowel team in each word.

Sound Bank

ai   ee   oa

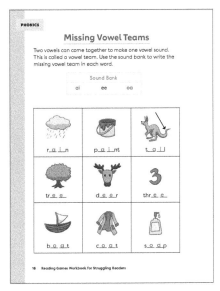

rain   paint   tail

tree   deer   three

boat   coat   soap

R-Controlled Vowels

Say these words with r-controlled vowels: **dark, horse, fork**. Circle the word with the r-controlled vowel that matches each picture.

Color by Digraphs

Some digraphs at the end of words are **ng, nk, ck, sh, th,** and **ch**. Use the key to color the picture.

Color Key

-ng   -ck   -th

-nk   -sh   -ch

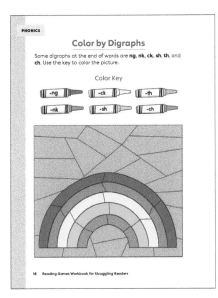

Soft C or Hard C?

A soft **C** makes the **s** sound. A hard **C** makes the **k** sound. Say each word. Listen for the hard **C** or soft **C**. Color the box with the matching sound.

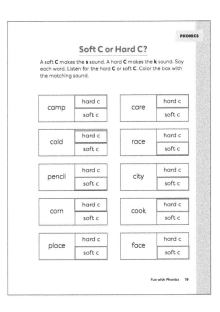

camp	hard c / soft c	care	hard c / soft c
cold	hard c / soft c	race	hard c / soft c
pencil	hard c / soft c	city	hard c / soft c
corn	hard c / soft c	cook	hard c / soft c
place	hard c / soft c	face	hard c / soft c

Soft G and Hard G

A soft **G** makes the **j** sound, like the beginning of **giant**.
A hard **G** makes the **g** sound, like the beginning of **gum**.
Draw a line through the words with soft **G** or hard **G** to make three in a row.

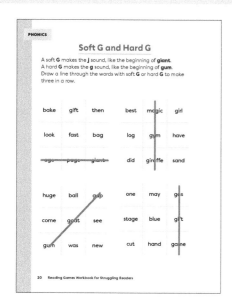

bake	gift	then		best	magic	girl
look	fast	bag		log	gym	have
age	page	giant		did	giraffe	sand
huge	ball	cup		one	may	gas
come	goat	see		stage	blue	gift
gum	was	new		cut	hand	game

Trigraph Search

A trigraph has three letters that make one sound, like **str** in the word **strap**. Find and circle the words with trigraphs in the puzzle.

Word Bank

scrape   splash   string
screw   spray   stretch

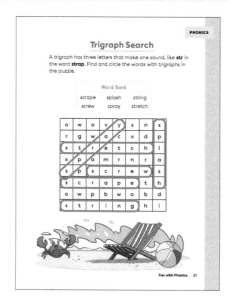

o	w	o	v	y	s	n	s
r	g	w	a	c	x	d	p
s	t	r	e	t	c	h	l
x	p	a	m	r	n	r	a
p	s	s	c	r	e	w	s
s	c	r	a	p	e	t	h
o	w	p	b	w	o	b	d
s	t	r	i	n	g	h	i

Follow the Diphthongs

A diphthong is a set of letters that makes two vowel sounds. Help the dragon get to the castle! Follow the words with diphthongs **oy**, **ou**, or **ow**.

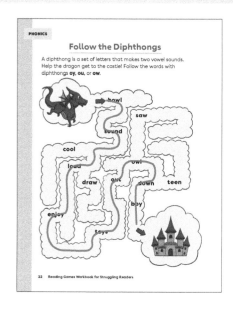

Double Consonants

Say these words with double consonants: **happy**, **puppy**, **penny**, **little**. Fill in the missing double consonants.

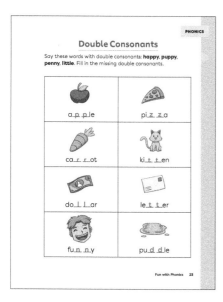

a_p_p_le	pi_z_za
ca_r_r_ot	ki_t_t_en
do_l_l_ar	le_t_t_er
fu_n_n_y	pu_d_d_le

Silent Letters

Silent letters are letters you do not hear when you say a word. Circle the words that have silent letters.

knock fist comb walk tree half drag hour bed wrist castle

What Sound?

The suffix **-ed** can sound like **t**, **d**, or **ed**. Say each word. Check the box with the matching **-ed** sound.

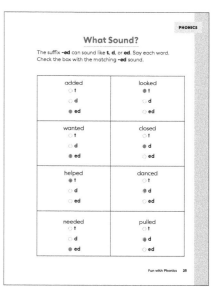

added	looked
○ t	● t
○ d	○ d
● ed	○ ed
wanted	closed
○ t	○ t
○ d	● d
● ed	○ ed
helped	danced
● t	○ t
○ d	● d
○ ed	○ ed
needed	pulled
○ t	○ t
○ d	● d
● ed	○ ed

Alliteration

Alliteration is when a group of words have the same beginning letter or sound. Read each sentence out loud. Write the beginning letter that is repeated.

Two turtles took turns.	T
Six silly snakes slithered slowly.	S
Five funny frogs flew far.	F
My mom makes macaroni.	M
We will walk with Wendy.	W

Sight Word Search

Sight words are the most common words you read and write. Find and circle the sight words in the puzzle.

Word Bank

this   we   than
as   she been

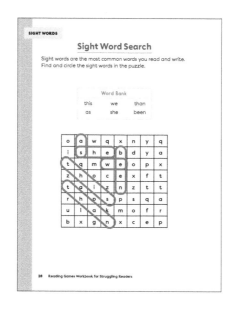

o	a	w	q	x	n	y	q
i	s	h	e	b	d	y	a
t	q	m	w	e	o	p	x
z	h	o	c	e	x	f	t
t	a	i	z	n	z	t	t
r	h	p	s	p	s	q	a
u	l	a	k	m	o	f	r
b	x	g	n	x	c	e	p

Tic-Tac-Toe

Some sight words only have two letters. Draw a line through the matching sight words to make three in a row.

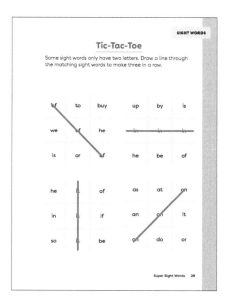

of	to	buy		up	by	is
we	of	he		in	in	in
is	or	of		he	be	of
he	it	of		as	at	on
in	it	if		an	on	it
so	it	be		on	do	or

---

108   **Answer Key**

Let's Go Skating!

Learning sight words will help you read. Help the skater get to the medal. Follow the sight words **more**, **there**, and **an**.

30   Reading Games Workbook for Struggling Readers

X Marks the Spot!

Consonants are letters that are not **A**, **E**, **I**, **O**, or **U**. Draw an **X** on the sight words that start with a consonant.

Super Sight Words   31

Blast Off!

You learn sight words by memorizing them. That means you don't have to sound them out. Use the key to color the picture.

Color Key

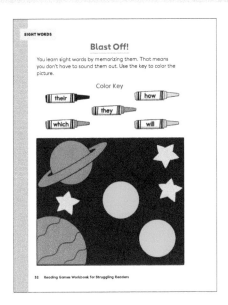

32   Reading Games Workbook for Struggling Readers

Trace and Match

Sight words can be tricky to spell. Tracing the letters can help you remember the spelling. Trace the words. Circle the matching word in each row.

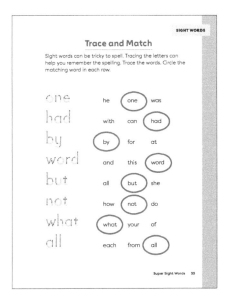

Super Sight Words   33

Find the Hidden Words

Reading a word over and over can help you memorize it. Use the word bank to find and circle the words.

Word Bank

other   many   people
about   number   them

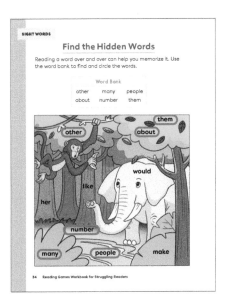

34   Reading Games Workbook for Struggling Readers

Find the Vowels

Most words have at least one vowel. Some have more than one. Vowels are the letters **A**, **E**, **I**, **O**, and **U**. Circle the vowels in each word.

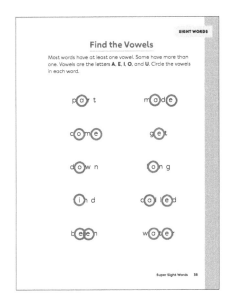

Super Sight Words   35

Missing Letters

Pictures can help you remember words. Look at each picture. Say the word. Fill in the missing letter.

rea d   c lock

l ook   firs t

b ack   t oy

36   Reading Games Workbook for Struggling Readers

Rainy Day Maze

Most syllables have only one vowel sound. Follow the words with one syllable to find your way home.

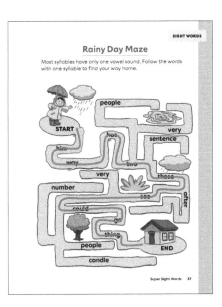

Super Sight Words   37

Scrambled Words

The letters in a scrambled word are mixed up in a different order. Use the word bank to unscramble the letters. Write the word.

tsju   just

kowr   work

nwok   know

mena   name

lhep   help

ames   same

nwat   want

sutm   must

Word Bank
must
help
know
just
work
want
name
same

38   Reading Games Workbook for Struggling Readers

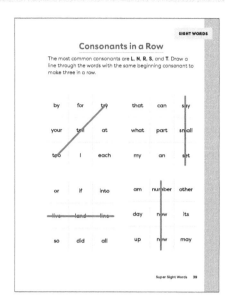

SIGHT WORDS

Consonants in a Row

The most common consonants are **L, N, R,** and **T.** Draw a line through the words with the same beginning consonant to make three in a row.

by	for	try	that	can	say
your	tell	at	what	part	small
too	I	each	my	an	set
or	if	into	am	number	other
live	land	line	day	now	its
so	did	all	up	new	may

Super Sight Words 39

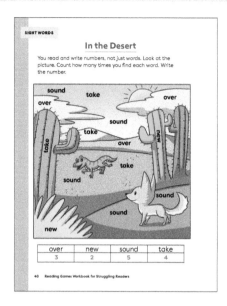

SIGHT WORDS

In the Desert

You read and write numbers, not just words. Look at the picture. Count how many times you find each word. Write the number.

over	new	sound	take
3	2	5	4

40 Reading Games Workbook for Struggling Readers

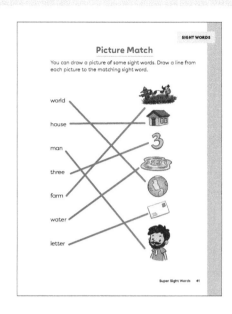

SIGHT WORDS

Picture Match

You can draw a picture of some sight words. Draw a line from each picture to the matching sight word.

world

house

man

three

farm

water

letter

Super Sight Words 41

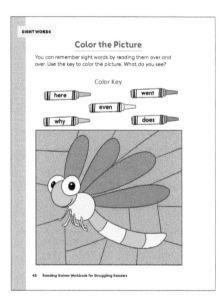

SIGHT WORDS

Color the Picture

You can remember sight words by reading them over and over. Use the key to color the picture. What do you see?

Color Key

here · went · even · why · does

42 Reading Games Workbook for Struggling Readers

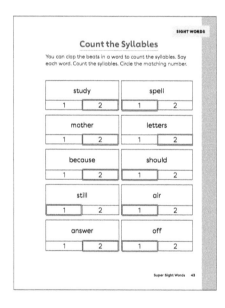

SIGHT WORDS

Count the Syllables

You can clap the beats in a word to count the syllables. Say each word. Count the syllables. Circle the matching number.

study		spell	
1	**2**	**1**	2
mother		letters	
1	**2**	1	**2**
because		should	
1	**2**	**1**	2
still		air	
1	2	**1**	2
answer		off	
1	**2**	**1**	2

Super Sight Words 43

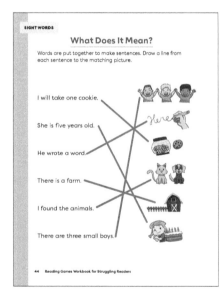

SIGHT WORDS

What Does It Mean?

Words are put together to make sentences. Draw a line from each sentence to the matching picture.

I will take one cookie.

She is five years old.

He wrote a word.

There is a farm.

I found the animals.

There are three small boys.

44 Reading Games Workbook for Struggling Readers

SIGHT WORDS

What Is Missing?

After you write a sentence, read it again to check that it makes sense. What word belongs in each sentence? Use the word bank to fill in the blanks.

Word Bank

think · Where · through
following · little · good

___Where___ will we go?

I will walk ___through___ the door.

What do you ___think___?

The puppy is ___following___ me.

This is a ___good___ idea.

The baby bird is ___little___

Super Sight Words 45

SIGHT WORDS

Sight Word Check

As you learn more sight words, you become an even better reader. Read the sight words. Circle the words you know. Memorize any words you do not know.

Answers may vary.

came	read	also	tell
line	then	some	great
old	any	before	help
want	show	around	means

48 Reading Games Workbook for Struggling Readers

SIGHT WORDS

Find the Sight Words

When you learn a new sight word, ask an adult to help you say it. Find and circle the sight words in the puzzle.

Word Bank

earn · page · away
kind · point · play

Super Sight Words 47

Panel 1 (top-left)

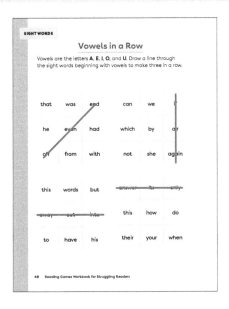

Vowels in a Row

Vowels are the letters **A, E, I, O,** and **U.** Draw a line through the sight words beginning with vowels to make three in a row.

that	was	end	can	we	if
he	even	had	which	by	or
off	from	with	not	she	again
this	words	but	answer	its	only
away	out	into	this	how	do
to	have	his	their	your	when

Panel 2 (top-middle)

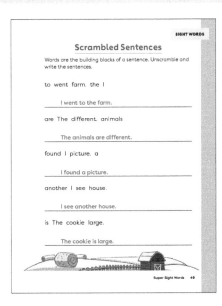

Scrambled Sentences

Words are the building blocks of a sentence. Unscramble and write the sentences.

to went farm. the I

I went to the farm.

are The different. animals

The animals are different.

found I picture. a

I found a picture.

another I see house.

I see another house.

is The cookie large.

The cookie is large.

Panel 3 (top-right)

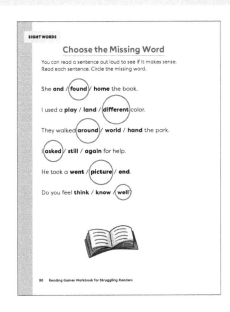

Choose the Missing Word

You can read a sentence out loud to see if it makes sense. Read each sentence. Circle the missing word.

She **and** / *found* / **home** the book.

I used a **play** / **land** / *different* color.

They walked *around* / **world** / **hand** the park.

I *asked* / **still** / *again* for help.

He took a **went** / *picture* / **end**.

Do you feel **think** / **know** / *well*?

Panel 4 (middle-left)

What Do You See?

You can show the meaning of a sentence with pictures. Draw a picture that matches each sentence.

Answers may vary.

The house is blue. | The boy can read.

I see the animals. | I write a sentence.

Panel 5 (middle-middle)

Building Fluency

Use the word bank to write the missing word in each sentence. Read the sentences out loud until you are reading with fluency.

Word Bank

America	us	again
change	went	following

I watched the movie ___again___

He will ___change___ his shirt.

The cat was ___following___ us.

This is a map of ___America___

Will you come with ___us___?

I ___went___ down the slide.

Panel 6 (middle-right)

Is It a Sentence?

A complete sentence will tell you what it is about and what is happening. Circle **yes** if the sentence is complete. Circle **no** if it is not a complete sentence.

my friend	yes	**no**
We went to the park.	**yes**	no
Played soccer.	yes	**no**
The kids	yes	**no**
They played tag.	**yes**	no
We had a picnic.	**yes**	no

Panel 7 (bottom-left)

Capitalize It!

A sentence always begins with a capital letter. Circle the letter that should be capitalized.

(l)et's go to the gym!

(w)e will play basketball.

(d)id you bring a basketball?

(t)here are four kids on our team.

(w)ho made a basket?

(w)e won the game!

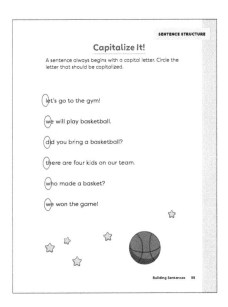

Panel 8 (bottom-middle)

Add the Ending

Punctuation marks have different uses. A period (.) is for a statement. A question mark (?) is for a question. An exclamation point (!) shows strong feeling. Add the right punctuation mark to complete each sentence.

Punctuation Marks

. ? !

Answers may vary.

Can we go to the zoo _?_

I am so excited to see the animals _!_

There are monkeys and lions _._

We can watch the zookeeper feed the seals _._

What time is the bird show _?_

Panel 9 (bottom-right)

Follow the Nouns

A noun is a person, place, or thing. Follow the nouns to help the turtle find the pond.

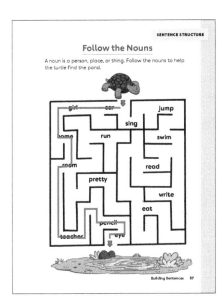

girl · cat · jump · sing · home · run · swim · room · read · pretty · write · eat · pencil · teacher · eye

Which Pronoun?

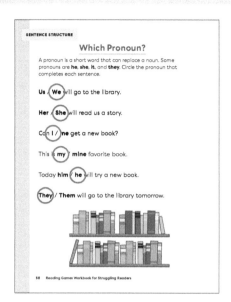

SENTENCE STRUCTURE

A pronoun is a short word that can replace a noun. Some pronouns are **he, she, it,** and **they.** Circle the pronoun that completes each sentence.

Us / (We) will go to the library.

Her / (She) will read us a story.

Can (I) / me get a new book?

This is (my) / mine favorite book.

Today him / (he) will try a new book.

(They) / Them will go to the library tomorrow.

58   Reading Games Workbook for Struggling Readers

Baking Up Verbs

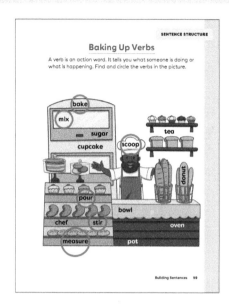

SENTENCE STRUCTURE

A verb is an action word. It tells you what someone is doing or what is happening. Find and circle the verbs in the picture.

Building Sentences   59

Find the Adjectives

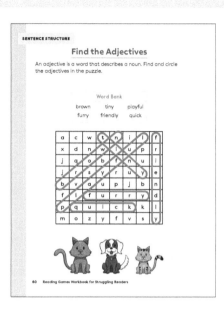

SENTENCE STRUCTURE

An adjective is a word that describes a noun. Find and circle the adjectives in the puzzle.

Word Bank

brown   tiny   playful
furry   friendly   quick

60   Reading Games Workbook for Struggling Readers

Connect the Verbs

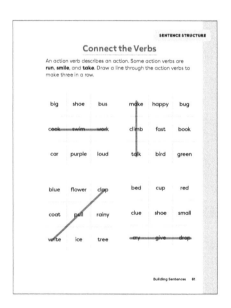

SENTENCE STRUCTURE

An action verb describes an action. Some action verbs are **run, smile,** and **take.** Draw a line through the action verbs to make three in a row.

big	shoe	bus	make	happy	bug
cook	swim	work	climb	fast	book
car	purple	loud	talk	bird	green

blue	flower	clap	bed	cup	red
coat	pull	rainy	clue	shoe	small
write	ice	tree	cry	give	drop

Building Sentences   61

Where Is the Cat?

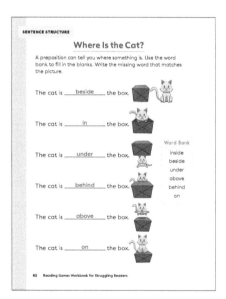

SENTENCE STRUCTURE

A preposition can tell you where something is. Use the word bank to fill in the blanks. Write the missing word that matches the picture.

The cat is ___beside___ the box.

The cat is ___in___ the box.

The cat is ___under___ the box.

The cat is ___behind___ the box.

The cat is ___above___ the box.

The cat is ___on___ the box.

Word Bank
inside
beside
under
above
behind
on

62   Reading Games Workbook for Struggling Readers

Describe It!

SENTENCE STRUCTURE

Adjectives can describe what something looks like. For example, an apple is red and round. Write two adjectives that describe each picture.

Answers may vary.

Building Sentences   63

My New Bike

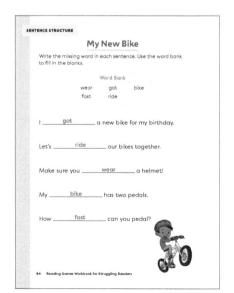

SENTENCE STRUCTURE

Write the missing word in each sentence. Use the word bank to fill in the blanks.

Word Bank
wear   got   bike
fast   ride

I ___got___ a new bike for my birthday.

Let's ___ride___ our bikes together.

Make sure you ___wear___ a helmet!

My ___bike___ has two pedals.

How ___fast___ can you pedal?

64   Reading Games Workbook for Struggling Readers

Let's Clean!

SENTENCE STRUCTURE

A sentence makes sense when the words are in order. Unscramble and write the sentences.

messy. My room is
            My room is messy.

clean room. I my will
            I will clean my room.

help Will me? you
            Will you help me?

stack my I books. will
            I will stack my books.

basket. clothes The in the go
            The clothes go in the basket.

clean! my Look at room
            Look at my clean room!

Building Sentences   65

Color the Nouns

SENTENCE STRUCTURE

A proper noun is a word that names a person, place, or thing. It begins with a capital letter. Use the key to color the picture.

Color Key
proper nouns
nouns

66   Reading Games Workbook for Struggling Readers

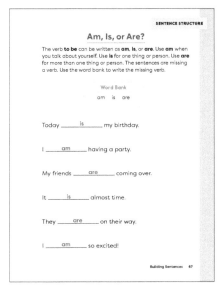

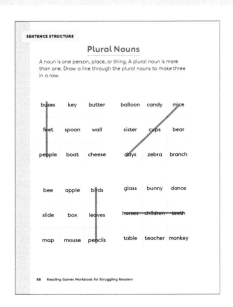

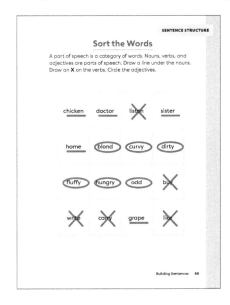

Am, Is, or Are?

The verb **to be** can be written as **am**, **is**, or **are**. Use **am** when you talk about yourself. Use **is** for one thing or person. Use **are** for more than one thing or person. The sentences are missing a verb. Use the word bank to write the missing verb.

Word Bank

am   is   are

Today ___is___ my birthday.

I ___am___ having a party.

My friends ___are___ coming over.

It ___is___ almost time.

They ___are___ on their way.

I ___am___ so excited!

Plural Nouns

A noun is one person, place, or thing. A plural noun is more than one. Draw a line through the plural nouns to make three in a row.

buses	key	butter	balloon	candy	mice
feet	spoon	wall	sister	cups	bear
people	boat	cheese	days	zebra	branch
bee	apple	birds	glass	bunny	dance
slide	box	leaves	horses	children	teeth
map	mouse	pencils	table	teacher	monkey

Sort the Words

A part of speech is a category of words. Nouns, verbs, and adjectives are parts of speech. Draw a line under the nouns. Draw an **X** on the verbs. Circle the adjectives.

chicken   doctor   listen(X)   sister

home   (blond)   (curvy)   (dirty)

(fluffy)   (hungry)   (odd)   buy(X)

write(X)   carry(X)   grape   like(X)

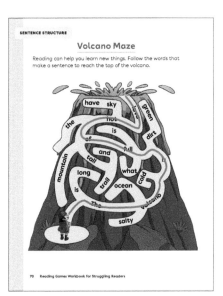

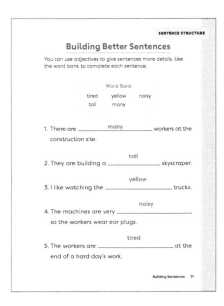

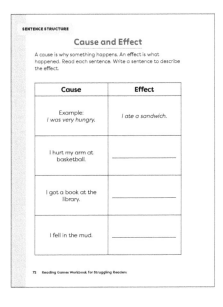

Volcano Maze

Reading can help you learn new things. Follow the words that make a sentence to reach the top of the volcano.

Building Better Sentences

You can use adjectives to give sentences more details. Use the word bank to complete each sentence.

Word Bank
tired   yellow   noisy
tall   many

1. There are ___many___ workers at the construction site.

2. They are building a ___tall___ skyscraper.

3. I like watching the ___yellow___ trucks.

4. The machines are very ___noisy___ so the workers wear ear plugs.

5. The workers are ___tired___ at the end of a hard day's work.

Cause and Effect

A cause is why something happens. An effect is what happened. Read each sentence. Write a sentence to describe the effect.

Cause	Effect
Example: I was very hungry.	I ate a sandwich.
I hurt my arm at basketball.	
I got a book at the library.	
I fell in the mud.	

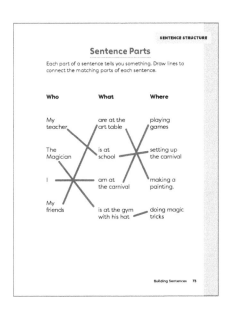

Sentence Parts

Each part of a sentence tells you something. Draw lines to connect the matching parts of each sentence.

Who	What	Where
My teacher	are at the art table	playing games
The Magician	is at school	setting up the carnival
I	am at the carnival	making a painting.
My friends	is at the gym with his hat	doing magic tricks

Scrambled Sentences

A sentence always ends with a punctuation mark. Unscramble and write the sentences.

do like best? sport What you
___What sport do you like best?___

play friends. with softball I my
___I play softball with my friends.___

called team My Lions. the is
___My team is called the Lions.___

the field. ball the I hit into will
___I will hit the ball into the field.___

you ball? catch the Can
___Can you catch the ball?___

won yesterday! team game Our the
___Our team won the game yesterday!___

Let's Go Fishing

A group of sentences can tell a story. Make a story about fishing. Circle the word that completes each sentence.

We went **skating** / **hiking** / (**fishing**) at the pond.

We used (**worms**) / **books** / **toys** for bait.

How many fish do you think we (**caught**) / **told** / **ran**?

We had to be **loud** / (**quiet**) / **happy** so we did not scare the fish.

We had a fun **party** / **breakfast** / (**day**)!

Answer Key   113

Music Class

You can read a sentence again to see if it makes sense. Use the word bank to complete each sentence. Read each sentence again. Does it make sense?

Word Bank

teacher   play   learning
today   music

Today we have _____music_____ class.

The _____teacher_____ tells us what to play.

I love _____learning_____ a new song each week.

Some days we get to _____play_____ instruments.

I wonder what we will do _____today_____!

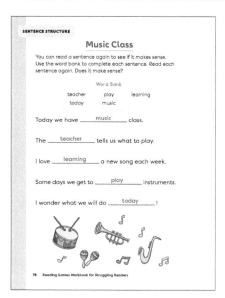

Cookout Fun!

A subject tells you who or what a sentence is about. A predicate tells you what happens. Draw a line from each subject to the matching predicate.

Subject   **Predicate**

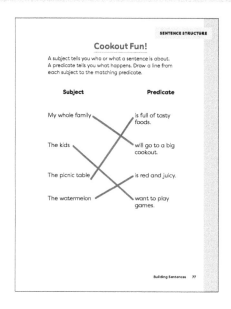

My whole family   is full of tasty foods.

The kids   will go to a big cookout.

The picnic table   is red and juicy.

The watermelon   want to play games.

Compound Scramble

A compound sentence has more than one predicate. The word **and** can be used to connect the predicates. Unscramble the predicates to write the compound sentences.

kicked I ball the	and	made goal. a
I kicked the ball	and	_made a goal._
dad My up woke	and	still sleepy. was
My dad woke up	and	_was still sleepy._
We movie watched a	and	ending. liked the
We watched a movie	and	_liked the ending._
made toast She	and	it. ate
She made toast	and	_ate it._

What Am I?

A riddle gives you clues to find an answer. Draw a line from each riddle to the matching picture.

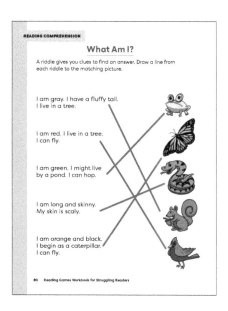

I am gray. I have a fluffy tail. I live in a tree.

I am red. I live in a tree. I can fly.

I am green. I might live by a pond. I can hop.

I am long and skinny. My skin is scaly.

I am orange and black. I begin as a caterpillar. I can fly.

Follow the Directions

A color word is the name of a color. Read each sentence with color words. Follow the directions to color the picture.

Color Key

Color two fish red.
Color one shell blue.
Color three starfish yellow.
Color two shells green.
Color one fish orange.

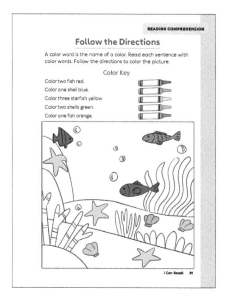

What Do You See?

Words and pictures can be used to tell a story. Read about the flower garden. Draw a picture to show what you read.

The garden is growing! I see three red flowers and two yellow flowers. There is a purple butterfly flying above the garden. I found a caterpillar crawling on green leaves. It is fun to look at the garden!

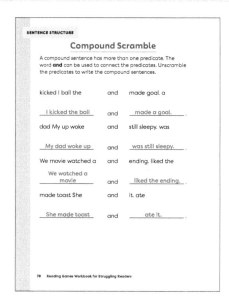

Answers will vary but should include the details from the story above

At the Zoo

As you read a story, each sentence tells you something new. Read each sentence. Draw a line to match it with the picture.

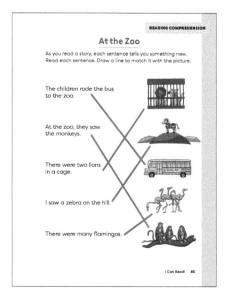

The children rode the bus to the zoo.

At the zoo, they saw the monkeys.

There were two lions in a cage.

I saw a zebra on the hill.

There were many flamingos.

Gray Wolves

A true statement is correct or right. A false statement is incorrect or wrong. Read about the gray wolf, then read the statements that follow. Write **true** or **false** next to each statement.

Have you ever seen a gray wolf? The gray wolf can be gray, brown, black, or even white! The colors help the wolf hide in nature. Gray wolves hunt at night. They work together as a pack to hunt bigger animals.

false   A gray wolf is always gray.

true   The gray wolf can hunt at night.

false   The colors make it hard for the wolf to hide.

false   Gray wolves only hunt small animals.

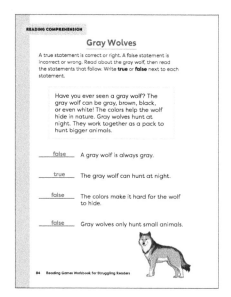

Making Connections

When you read something new, you can connect it to something you already know. Read about the apple orchard. Use the questions to help you write about your own connection to the story.

Our class went on a field trip to the apple orchard. The workers taught us how they grow the trees. We got to pick apples. We even tasted apples! My favorite apple was red and sweet.

Answers will vary but should reflect a connection the reader can make with apples or a trip to the apple orchard.

Have you been to an apple orchard?

_____

Have you gone on a field trip?

_____

Do you like apples?

_____

Main Idea

The main idea of a story tells you what the story is about. Read the story about llamas. Think about the main idea as you read.

> Llamas are very smart animals. They can be trained to do many things. Llamas can learn to pull a cart. They help farmers carry heavy things. Llamas also work as guard animals.

The main idea is:

_____ Answers will vary but should be _____
_____ about llamas being smart. _____
_____
_____
_____
_____
_____

What You Know

Background knowledge is what you already know before you read. Use your background knowledge about butterflies. Write what you already know about them. Then read the story that follows to an adult.

What I know about butterflies:

_____ Answers will vary but should include _____
_____ knowledge about butterflies. _____
_____
_____
_____

Amy loves to watch butterflies! They are her favorite insect. She likes how they start as a caterpillar and become a butterfly. Do you have a favorite insect?

_____ Answers will vary but should be _____
_____ about an insect. _____
_____
_____

Name That Food

Riddles are sometimes called brain teasers. This is because you use your brain to solve them. Draw a line to match each riddle with the picture.

I am baked in the oven. I have cheese and tomato sauce.

I am yellow. I have a peel.

I am round and sweet. I have a hole in the middle.

I am a fruit. I am red and crunchy.

I am made from potatoes. I am salty and crispy.

I have a tortilla on the outside. I have meat and beans.

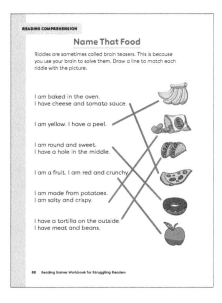

What Will Damian Do?

A prediction is when you use clues to guess what will happen. Read about Damian. Make a prediction about what will happen.

> Damian looked outside. It was snowing! He put on his coat, boots, gloves, and a hat. He found his sled in the garage. Then he walked up the hill next to his house.

What do you think Damian will do next?

_____ Answers will vary. _____
_____
_____
_____
_____
_____
_____
_____
_____

Getting Ready

When you do not know a word, you can ask an adult for help. Read about the road trip. Circle any words you do not know and ask an adult. Then read the passage out loud.

> My family woke up early to get ready for our road trip. First, we packed our bags. Next, we packed a cooler with food. We put everything into the car. It was time to start our adventure!

Circled words will vary.

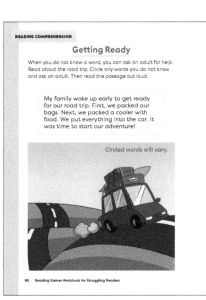

Giant Pandas

A fact is a statement that can be proven true or false. An opinion is a belief or feeling. Opinions are not true or false. Read each statement. Write **F** if it is a fact. Write **O** if it is an opinion.

___O___ Giant pandas are so fun to watch!

___F___ They are a type of bear.

___F___ Giant pandas are found in China.

___F___ Their diet is mostly bamboo.

___O___ All zoos should have giant pandas.

A Trip to the Ice Cream Shop

Sequencing is when you put sentences in order to tell a story. Read each sentence. Write the numbers **1** to **5** to put the sentences in order.

___3___ She put the ice cream scoop on a cone.

___4___ She handed me the cone.

___1___ I ordered chocolate ice cream.

___5___ I tasted the ice cream, and it was delicious!

___2___ The worker scooped the ice cream.

Making Predictions

Words are clues that help you make a prediction. Read the story. Write one or two sentences to predict what will happen next.

> My mom told me to get my swimsuit and sunglasses. She put sunscreen on me and my brother. We put towels, buckets, and shovels in the car.

_____ Answers should reference _____
_____ going to the beach. _____
_____
_____
_____
_____
_____
_____
_____

The Purpose of Writing

Writing has different purposes. It can **entertain**, **persuade**, and **inform**. Entertain is when you amuse. Persuade is when you to try to make someone believe an idea. Inform is when you teach. Why would the author write each of these books? Fill in the circle next to the matching purpose.

The Magical Unicorn	Why You Should Play Basketball
● entertain	○ entertain
○ persuade	● persuade
○ inform	○ inform
All about Penguins	Desert Animals
○ entertain	○ entertain
○ persuade	○ persuade
● inform	● inform
The Birthday Party Adventure	Why You Should Get a Cat
● entertain	○ entertain
○ persuade	● persuade
○ inform	○ inform

Answer Key   **115**

Learn by Reading

Reading can help us learn about the world. Read about the maned sloth. Write **true** or **false** next to the statements that follow.

> The maned sloth lives in Brazil. It has thick, brown hair. Sloths like hot and humid weather. They live in trees where they can sleep up to 20 hours each day! Their favorite food is leaves.

True or False?

___T___ The maned sloth has brown hair.

___F___ The maned sloth likes snowy weather.

___F___ The maned sloth only sleeps three hours a day.

___T___ The maned sloth likes to eat leaves.

The Walk

Words can be shown in pictures. Read the story. Draw a picture to show what happened in the story.

> When I went for a walk with my sister, I saw a bird in a tree. The bird was big and blue. It was sitting in a nest. There were four tiny eggs in the nest. I loved watching the bird on this sunny day!

Answers will vary but should show a picture of a bird.

Reading Vocabulary

You learn different skills when you read. Draw a line from each reading skill to the matching definition.

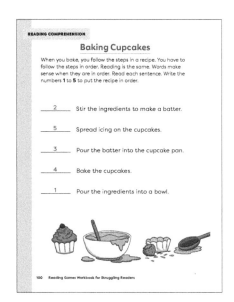

prediction — the reason an author writes

fact — a belief

purpose — when a reader uses clues to figure out what will happen next

connection — being able to read easily

opinion — when we use what we already know to help us read

fluency — a statement that can be proven

Where Am I?

Reading and answering riddles can be like solving a mystery. Use the word bank to answer the riddles.

Word Bank

school   forest   beach
zoo   desert

___beach___ I have sand and salty water.

___zoo___ I have many animals. They might live in cages or behind a fence.

___forest___ I have lots of trees. You can find birds, squirrels, and deer in me.

___desert___ I am very dry. You might see a cactus or a snake if you visit me.

___school___ You will see books, pencils, and teachers here.

Narwhals

A paragraph is a group of sentences. Read about narwhals. Then read the questions. Underline the answers in the paragraph. Write the answers.

> A narwhal is a whale. It has a tusk on its head. This makes narwhals look like unicorns that swim! Narwhals live in icy ocean waters. They eat fish, shrimp, and squid.

What makes a narwhal look like a unicorn?

_____a tusk_____

Where do narwhals live?

_____icy ocean waters_____

What are two foods that narwhals eat?

___answers should include fish, shrimp, or squid___

Baking Cupcakes

When you bake, you follow the steps in a recipe. You have to follow the steps in order. Reading is the same. Words make sense when they are in order. Read each sentence. Write the numbers **1** to **5** to put the recipe in order.

___2___ Stir the ingredients to make a batter.

___5___ Spread icing on the cupcakes.

___3___ Pour the batter into the cupcake pan.

___4___ Bake the cupcakes.

___1___ Pour the ingredients into a bowl.

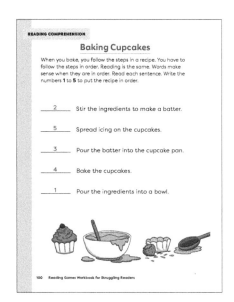

Why Did the Author Write This?

Read about Power Shoes. Think about why this was written.

> Have you seen Power Shoes? They are the best shoes you will ever own. They will help you jump high and run fast. Plus, they look great. You should buy a pair today!

Why do you think the author wrote this?

Answers may vary but could be: The author is writing to persuade the reader to buy Power Shoes.

Retelling a Story

A story has a beginning, middle, and end. Read the story about a camping trip. Draw pictures to show the beginning, middle, and end of the story.

> Kendall and Carter are going camping! First, they will pitch their tent. Next, they will build a campfire. Finally, they are going to cook dinner. They will have a fun night!

Beginning

Middle — Drawings will vary; beginning drawing should include pitching a tent, middle drawing should include building a fire, and the end drawing should include two people cooking.

End

Making a Summary

A summary tells the main idea of a story. Read the paragraph. Make a summary of what you read by explaining the main idea and writing three details.

> My class went to the museum on our field trip. My favorite part of the museum had dinosaur fossils. We talked with a paleontologist. A paleontologist is a scientist who learns about dinosaurs by studying fossils. We learned that dinosaurs are reptiles that lived a long time ago. Did you know that some dinosaurs had feathers like birds? I learned so much on our trip!

What is the main idea?

Answers may vary but could be: The child enjoyed the dinosaur fossils at the museum.

Write three details.

1. ___Answers may vary but should___
2. ___be in the paragraph above.___
3. _____

---

116   Answer Key